The Unspoken Side
From Kim's Lost Words

Detailed Story Behind the Relationship of
Kimberly Porter and Sean Combs, Including
Allegations of Abuse from Her Memoir

Evelyn Everlore

TABLE OF CONTENT

INTRODUCTION

Kim Porter was a model, actress, and philanthropist, but more importantly, she was known for her strength, grace, and deep love for her family. As the mother of three of Sean "Diddy" Combs' children, she led a life in the public eye, balancing fame with the role of a devoted mother. Her passing in 2018 left a significant impact on the entertainment world, and her legacy continues to inspire many, emphasizing resilience, compassion, and the importance of personal strength in overcoming challenges.

The purpose of this book is to honor Kim Porter's life by exploring her untold story, one that goes beyond the tabloid headlines. Through reflections on her personal struggles, achievements, and enduring love for her children, this book aims to provide a deeper understanding of Kim as more than just a public figure. It focuses on her resilience, strength, and the lessons her life offers for anyone navigating love, family, and personal growth. This book serves as a tribute, preserving her memory and offering insight into the woman behind the fame.

CHAPTER 1

Kim Porter's Early Life and Career

Family and Early Aspirations

Born and raised in Columbus, Georgia, Kim Porter grew up in a supportive family that nurtured her early ambitions. As a teenager, she developed a passion for modeling, balancing her youthful dreams with the expectations placed upon her as a debutante in her local community. After graduating from Columbus High School in 1988, she set out to pursue a career in fashion and entertainment. Her determination led her to move to Atlanta, Georgia, where she would begin her professional journey, breaking into the modeling industry and soon after transitioning into acting.

Modeling and Acting Career Highlights

Kim's career took off after relocating to Atlanta, where she quickly established herself as a talented and hardworking model. Her striking presence earned her features in several high-profile music videos, which showcased her beauty and versatility. It wasn't long before she transitioned into acting, securing roles in films such as *The Brothers* (2001) and *Mama, I Want to Sing!* (2012), and starring in TV series like *Wicked Wicked Games* (2006–2007) and *Single Ladies* (2011).

Throughout her career, Kim balanced various creative pursuits, including co-founding "Three Brown Girls," a lifestyle planning company based in Atlanta. She, alongside college friends Nicole Cooke-Johnson and Eboni Elektra, helped promote rising talent in the entertainment industry, most notably playing a key role in the early career of singer Janelle Monáe. Kim's belief in Monáe's potential proved to be a turning point for the artist, who has since spoken about her gratitude for Kim's support.

In addition to her modeling and acting accomplishments, Kim also worked as a receptionist at Uptown Records, where she was hired by the legendary Andre Harrell. Her time at Uptown would further solidify her connections within the music industry and lay the foundation for the public figure she would later become. Kim's early career was marked by determination, an eye for opportunity, and an unwavering belief in the power of creativity and collaboration.

CHAPTER 2

Life with Diddy

Public Image of Their Relationship

Kim Porter and Sean "Diddy" Combs were one of the most iconic couples in the entertainment industry. Their relationship was highly publicized, with the media often portraying them as a glamorous, larger-than-life couple, reflecting the epitome of the hip-hop and celebrity lifestyle. Despite numerous ups and downs, their bond remained one of the most enduring relationships in the entertainment world.

Kim and Diddy's relationship spanned decades, beginning in the 1990s. They had an on-and-off dynamic, with several public breakups and reconciliations, which only fueled public fascination. Despite the challenges, they were consistently seen at events together, exuding a sense of unity and support for each other's careers. Whether attending high-profile award shows or being photographed on vacation, the world viewed their relationship as both aspirational and tumultuous.

However, the public image only scratched the surface. Behind the scenes, their relationship had its share of struggles. But what remained constant throughout was Kim's ability to maintain her own sense of identity and purpose, even while being in a relationship with one of the most powerful figures in the music industry.

Motherhood and Family Life

Perhaps the most important role in Kim's life was that of a mother. She and Diddy shared three children: Christian, and twin daughters D'Lila Star and Jessie James. Kim was also a mother to Quincy, her son from a previous relationship with singer Al B. Sure!, whom Diddy adopted as his own. Motherhood was central to Kim's life, and she often spoke of her children with immense pride and love.

Kim was known for creating a loving and supportive home environment for her children. Despite Diddy's busy career and the pressures of fame, Kim was the rock that held the family together. She ensured that her children stayed grounded, nurturing their talents while shielding them from the excesses of the celebrity world. Kim was involved in every aspect of their lives, from school to extracurricular activities, to guiding them in their own creative pursuits.

Even as she juggled a successful career, Kim remained a devoted mother who cherished her time with her children. She frequently shared family moments, instilling values of kindness, humility, and the importance of strong family bonds. Many in her circle admired her ability to balance her public life with her deeply private and intimate role as a mother.

Kim and Diddy's family life was complex but filled with love. Although they eventually parted ways romantically, their bond as co-parents remained strong. Kim and Diddy were united in their efforts to raise their children, often celebrating holidays and special moments together. Their blended family was a testament to Kim's dedication to fostering unity and love among all her children, regardless of the ups and downs of her personal relationship with Diddy.

Kim's ability to maintain this delicate balance between fame and family is one of her most enduring legacies. She was more than just a celebrity partner—she was a mother, a friend, and a grounding force for those around her. Her family life and her devotion to her children are key aspects of her legacy, making her a beloved figure not only in the public eye but also within her family's inner circle.

CHAPTER 3

Challenges and Triumphs

Personal Struggles Behind the Scenes

Behind Kim Porter's glamorous public persona, she faced numerous personal struggles that she managed to keep private. One of the most significant challenges was her on-and-off relationship with Diddy, marked by emotional highs and lows. While they were often seen as the ultimate power couple, Kim faced difficulties balancing the pressure of being in a high-profile relationship with her desire for personal peace and stability. Their relationship was tumultuous at times, with breakups and reconciliations often playing out in the media, adding further stress to her personal life.

Additionally, Kim dealt with the demands of motherhood while trying to carve out a career for herself. As a model, actress, and entrepreneur, she had aspirations beyond being seen as Diddy's partner. However, balancing her personal ambitions with the responsibilities of raising four children was a challenge that required immense strength and resilience. She was often tasked with ensuring her family remained grounded despite the chaotic world of fame and fortune they lived in.

Kim also faced health challenges that were not widely publicized. Despite her seemingly flawless image, she endured private struggles that she kept from the public eye, showing how strong she was as she continued to persevere through adversity. Her ability to maintain a steady and calm demeanor while dealing with these internal conflicts made her a figure of admiration to those who knew her intimately.

Kim's Personal Growth

Through her challenges, Kim Porter demonstrated significant personal growth. Over the years, she evolved from a model and actress into a resilient, self-assured woman with a strong sense of identity. Even with the pressures of being Diddy's partner, Kim consistently worked to establish herself as more than just a "celebrity girlfriend"—she was an entrepreneur, a loving mother, and a woman determined to live life on her own terms.

One of the most prominent aspects of Kim's growth was her ability to create and maintain strong bonds of friendship and loyalty. She was known for her unwavering support of her friends and family, often putting the needs of others ahead of her own. Her involvement in launching the careers of talents like Janelle Monáe through her lifestyle planning company, *Three Brown Girls*, is a testament to her growth as a mentor and visionary. Through her efforts, Kim fostered an environment of empowerment for others, believing in their potential when others might have overlooked them.

As she matured, Kim also learned to prioritize her well-being, recognizing the importance of self-care and self-worth. Even though she remained linked to Diddy in the public eye, she made efforts to carve out her own space in the world. Her personal triumphs extended beyond her career and into her role as a mother, where she demonstrated incredible patience and wisdom in raising her children with values of humility and kindness, despite the privileges that came with fame.

Kim's personal growth was not just about her professional achievements but about finding balance, peace, and purpose amidst the chaos of the celebrity world. She developed an inner strength that allowed her to navigate her personal struggles with grace and dignity, ultimately leaving behind a legacy of resilience, compassion, and empowerment. Through it all, Kim's ability to grow from her challenges and transform them into triumphs is what defined her not just as a public figure but as an extraordinary human being.

Her life's journey of overcoming hardships, learning from her experiences, and emerging stronger serves as an inspiration for anyone facing personal struggles. Kim's story is one of perseverance, proving that growth can come from the most challenging of circumstances.

CHAPTER 4

A Life of Love and Friendship

Relationships with Friends and Family

Kim Porter was known not only for her public life but for her deeply cherished personal relationships. Throughout her life, Kim nurtured close bonds with her friends and family, which served as the foundation of her world. She was a loyal and dedicated friend, maintaining long-lasting friendships with those who supported and loved her unconditionally. These relationships were not just built on the glamour of the entertainment industry but were rooted in genuine love, trust, and shared experiences.

Among her closest friends were those she co-founded *Three Brown Girls* with, Nicole Cooke-Johnson and Eboni Elektra. This company not only helped launch careers but also symbolized Kim's commitment to empowering others, particularly women of color, to thrive in their careers and personal lives. Her friendships were a testament to her character—loyal, supportive, and always willing to lend a helping hand or a kind word to those in need.

In her family, Kim played a pivotal role as the glue that held everyone together. As a daughter, sister, and cousin, she remained close to her roots in Columbus, Georgia, where her family took pride in her success, knowing that despite her fame, she remained grounded. Her family described her as warm, compassionate, and fiercely protective of her loved ones. Kim's ability to maintain strong familial ties while navigating the complexities of fame speaks volumes about her character.

Role as a Mother and Caregiver

At the heart of Kim Porter's life was her role as a mother. Her children—Quincy, Christian, and twin daughters D'Lila Star and Jessie James—were her pride and joy. Kim was deeply committed to being present in their lives, ensuring they were raised with love, discipline, and a sense of responsibility. She made it a priority to shield them from the pressures of the entertainment industry, striving to create a nurturing and normal environment despite the fame that surrounded their family.

Kim's parenting style was hands-on and rooted in love. She was the type of mother who attended every school function, extracurricular activity, and important event in her children's lives. She worked tirelessly to ensure that they had everything they needed, not just materially but emotionally as well. Her home was a sanctuary of warmth and love, where her children knew they could always count on her for support.

Even as she faced her own personal challenges, Kim remained devoted to her children's well-being. Her role as a caregiver extended beyond her own kids—Kim was also a maternal figure to many of her friends and those in her community. She often opened her home to those in need of advice, support, or simply a shoulder to lean on. Her nurturing nature made her not only a mother to her biological children but a guiding force for many others as well.

Kim's relationship with Diddy, despite its ups and downs, was always centered around their children. Even after they parted ways romantically, Kim and

Diddy remained united in their goal of raising their children in a loving environment. They often came together to celebrate holidays and family milestones, showcasing Kim's unwavering dedication to co-parenting and maintaining a positive atmosphere for her kids.

In every aspect of her life, Kim's love for her family and friends was evident. She created a legacy not just through her professional achievements, but through the profound impact she had on the people closest to her. Kim's life was a life of love, and her relationships with those around her reflected the kindness and compassion she embodied. She was a caregiver in every sense of the word—one who gave her heart and soul to those she loved, leaving behind a legacy of love and friendship that will endure for generations to come.

CHAPTER 5

Details From The Posthumous Memoir - KIM'S LOST WORDS

The new 60-page book "Kim's Lost Words" is reportedly based on Kim Porter's alleged diaries and details her relationship with Sean "Diddy" Combs from the 1990s until her death. The book, published by Chris Todd under the pseudonym Jamal T. Millwood, claims Porter wrote about Diddy's personal life, including their open relationship, allegations of abuse, and controversial incidents involving celebrities. Todd claims to have received a flash drive with Porter's writings, but no documentary proof has been provided. Some of Porter's friends deny the existence of such diaries and have labeled the book exploitative.

The book also includes claims of alleged encounters between Diddy and young pop stars, as well as shocking revelations about parties. According to Todd, these diary entries were shared by friends of Porter and include details about Diddy's alleged abusive behavior, including a reported violent altercation. Porter allegedly kept copies of videos she discovered in Diddy's possession as protection, which later became part of the memoir's most sensational claims.

Todd admitted that he initially withheld his name from the book for security reasons, but decided to come forward after Diddy's recent legal issues. However, the book's lack of verification has raised doubts about its authenticity. Porter's close friend, Eboni Elektra, has publicly denied the existence of the diaries and criticized the memoir for profiting from Kim's memory. Todd has also shared a photo of Porter allegedly taken after one of Diddy's attacks, but these claims have not been substantiated.

The book continues to stir controversy, with many urging authorities to investigate further. However, without concrete evidence to support its claims, "Kim's Lost Words" remains highly disputed.

How Authentic is This Memoir?

Concerns about the authenticity of *Kim's Lost Words* have been growing, as no solid evidence has been presented to prove the legitimacy of the alleged diaries. While the book continues to generate attention and is available for purchase, skepticism remains. Kim Porter's close friend, Eboni Elektra, publicly denounced the book on Instagram, emphatically stating that Kim never wrote such a memoir. She criticized both the media and the publishers for profiting off of falsehoods and exploiting Kim's memory, urging the public to respect the truth about her life.

What Next?

Without any verification and considering the strong denial from Kim Porter's close friend, "Kim's Lost Words" raises more questions than answers. Publisher Chris Todd's vague connection to the material, along with the timing of the book's release, makes many skeptical of its legitimacy. Eboni Elektra, a close confidante of Kim, has publicly debunked the memoir's existence, calling it a sensationalized attempt to profit from falsehoods. While it may attract attention, it's important to approach such claims with caution and recognize the lack of credible evidence backing the story.

Details of The Allegations

Some of the alleged scandals in "Kim's Lost Words" claim that in 1999, Diddy was involved in a nightclub shooting where rapper Shyne took the fall. Although Diddy and then-girlfriend Jennifer Lopez were also arrested, only Shyne faced charges, with rumors circulating about Diddy's responsibility ever since. The memoir also accuses Diddy of hosting lavish parties that were reportedly orgies, though many participants have denied these claims.

The book *Kim's Lost Words* contains numerous sensational claims about the relationship between Kim Porter and Sean "Diddy" Combs. It alleges their sex life included threesomes, partner-swapping, and open relationships. One specific claim suggests that Porter was involved with a well-known married woman, while Diddy was reportedly with a chart-topping rapper and the woman's husband. The memoir goes further to suggest that Porter and Diddy had an open relationship, with Porter reportedly having relationships with the late rapper Tupac Shakur.

One of the most disturbing incidents mentioned in the memoir claims that Diddy first hit Porter after she refused to fulfill one of his sexual requests. The narrative continues with Porter allegedly describing how Diddy asked her to engage in certain acts, which led to a violent encounter. According to the book, after the first instance of violence, Diddy supposedly hit Porter hard, only to quickly apologize afterward. This incident left her shaken but, as she admitted, she felt conflicted about leaving the relationship at that point.

The book also details another violent incident in Porter's apartment, where Diddy allegedly slammed her to the ground and brandished a .22 caliber handgun, placing it on a table. In this situation, Diddy reportedly knelt in front of her, professing that she was his and she had no choice in the matter, claiming he couldn't live without her. Porter allegedly characterized him as a "terrifying monster" after this incident, revealing how much fear and control she felt during their time together.

One of the more shocking claims from the memoir involves video tapes of Diddy's sexual encounters. According to the book, Porter discovered and copied these tapes as a form of protection. When she reviewed them, she was reportedly disturbed by the content, which included not just sexual activity with male and female partners but also underage boys. The memoir goes so far as to mention specific individuals, including famous musicians who were allegedly involved in these tapes. Porter reportedly expressed shock and disgust upon discovering these recordings, especially given the youth of some of the individuals involved.

The memoir's publisher, Chris Todd, claimed that friends of both Porter and Diddy had access to these tapes and had been shopping them around to Hollywood producers. Todd himself reportedly had access to the tapes, though no clear evidence has emerged to validate these claims. He even suggested that parties involved in these tapes had been approached with offers to sell them for documentary purposes, although he did not disclose whether any deals had been finalized.

Todd also shared a photograph, allegedly of Kim Porter, taken in her bathroom in her Toluca Lake mansion around 2009. The photo, according to Todd, was taken by a friend of Porter's and showed her applying makeup to cover up an injury from one of Diddy's alleged physical assaults. The background of the photo reportedly matched images of the bathroom in the mansion where Porter was found dead in 2018, adding a somber and tragic layer to the narrative surrounding her life and death.

Although these claims have been made, it's important to note that no substantial evidence has been provided to verify the events described in *Kim's Lost Words*. Todd has admitted to withholding his identity at first for safety reasons but has now come forward following Diddy's legal troubles, suggesting that he feels safer in revealing these details. Nonetheless, without documentary proof, these allegations remain speculative and have been met with skepticism by many, especially those close to Porter who have publicly denied the existence of such diaries.

The book's release has stirred controversy, but the lack of tangible evidence and the denial from Kim Porter's close friends make it difficult to assess the truth behind these claims. The allegations presented in *Kim's Lost Words* are undoubtedly disturbing, yet without further corroboration, they exist in the murky territory between scandal and speculation.

CHAPTER 6

The Dramatic Fall of Sean 'Diddy' Combs"

Sean "Diddy" Combs, once one of the most celebrated figures in American entertainment, is now confined to the Metropolitan Detention Center (MDC) in Brooklyn. His once-dazzling empire, built on hip-hop stardom, fashion, and luxury, has crumbled under the weight of severe criminal charges. Just a few miles from where his protege, Biggie Smalls, grew up, and far from his middle-class roots in Mount Vernon, Combs' current reality starkly contrasts his previous life of opulence.

Once a dominant force in both music and fashion, Combs paraded his wealth through extravagant parties, luxury yachts, and private jets. He epitomized the era of "bling," where indulgence and grandeur ruled. Combs' business ventures, from his fashion line Sean John to his Cîroc vodka partnership, built a formidable brand, symbolizing the fusion of hip-hop culture and luxury consumerism. At his peak, he was the king of opulent living, celebrated for bringing hip-hop into mainstream luxury. As *Vibe* editor Alan Light put it, Diddy connected hip-hop to "a different kind of glamour and aspiration."

But all that came crashing down. Combs' wealth and influence could not protect him from a dramatic fall when, in 2024, a New York judge denied him a $50 million bail package, citing concerns of witness tampering. Now facing multiple charges, including racketeering conspiracy, sex trafficking, and transportation for prostitution, the former mogul faces the possibility of decades behind bars.

The federal indictment against Combs is not just about his alleged personal conduct, but the systemized criminal activities he is accused of orchestrating. U.S. Attorney Damian Williams claimed Combs used his business empire to facilitate forced labor, sex trafficking, and other illicit activities, allegations reminiscent of notorious cases like those of Jeffrey Epstein and R. Kelly. From alleged "freak off" parties fueled by drugs and debauchery to coerced sexual performances, the charges paint a deeply disturbing picture of Combs' actions behind closed doors. Prosecutors allege that he not only exploited women but also transported individuals across state lines for illegal purposes, turning what might seem like a personal scandal into a federal case.

Legal experts like Anna Cominsky, director of New York Law School's criminal defense clinic, have pointed out the gravity of the racketeering charge. Combs' case isn't just about him—it's about an organized network that enabled these alleged crimes. Racketeering cases often rely on co-conspirators turning into cooperating witnesses, which may spell further trouble for Combs. As Cominsky remarked, "co-conspirators don't have to be charged and are often turned into cooperating witnesses," a strategy that could amplify the severity of Combs' case.

As the case unfolds, it's notable how few of Combs' former associates or high-profile friends have stepped forward to support him—a pattern seen in other cases of powerful men like Epstein and Harvey Weinstein. Even public figures like Charlamagne Tha God have predicted that more people involved in Combs' activities may face legal consequences. Rapper 50 Cent, never shy about criticizing his industry peers, made a pointed remark about the accusations against Combs, while singer Aubrey O'Day expressed a sense of "validation" at his arrest, viewing it as a win for women everywhere.

Combs' defense team, led by Marc Agnifilo, maintains that their client is innocent, asserting that "there's no coercion and no crime." They proposed a stringent bail package, including home detention and drug tests, but the court remained unconvinced. Judge Andrew L. Carter Jr. expressed concern not about Combs' potential to flee, but about the risk of obstruction of justice, particularly witness intimidation. Witness tampering allegations further complicate Combs' legal standing, making his path to freedom an uphill battle.

The 14-page indictment outlines the government's charges against Combs, but the investigation is ongoing. Prosecutors have hinted that additional individuals may be implicated, though whether these individuals will face charges or cooperate with authorities remains to be seen. Cominsky warned that co-conspirators often become key witnesses in cases like this, possibly worsening the situation for Combs as the trial progresses.

The roots of Combs' troubled trajectory go far back. Despite his image as a business genius, there were signs of trouble early in his career. In 1991, seven people were killed during a stampede at a celebrity basketball game he had organized. A decade later, Combs was arrested after a nightclub shooting, though he was later cleared of charges. These incidents hinted at a darker side beneath his glamorous exterior.

As his criminal trial moves forward, many are reflecting on how Combs managed to maintain such an elaborate facade of success while allegedly engaging in illegal activities. Combs' carefully curated public image is now under scrutiny, with some questioning how these behaviors remained hidden in plain sight for so long. As Cominsky notes, racketeering cases take time to build, and while it might seem that his prosecution took longer than expected, the complex nature of these investigations requires patience and careful planning from prosecutors.

While his defense team continues to fight, the weight of the charges and the number of witnesses involved make Combs' battle for freedom a daunting one. For a man whose life was once defined by glamour, influence, and fame, the stakes could not be higher. The fall of Sean "Diddy" Combs serves as a stark reminder of how quickly fortunes can change, and how even those at the top are not immune to the consequences of their actions.

Detailed Explanations of The Charges Against Sean 'Diddy' Combs

Cassie's Lawsuit

On November 16, 2023, singer and model Cassie, also known as Casandra Ventura, filed a lawsuit against Sean "Diddy" Combs, alleging he exploited his power to manipulate and coerce her into an abusive relationship. The lawsuit detailed violent abuse, with claims that Combs regularly assaulted her, leaving her with injuries. Cassie also described "freak offs," drug-fueled parties where women were coerced into performing sexual acts. Combs denied the allegations, accusing Cassie of extortion. The lawsuit was settled for an undisclosed amount the day after it was filed, with Combs maintaining his innocence.

More Lawsuits Allege Sexual Assault

In the weeks following the settlement of Cassie's lawsuit, Sean "Diddy" Combs faced additional sexual assault accusations from multiple women. One anonymous woman alleged that Combs and another man coerced her into sex. Joi Dickerson-Neal claimed he drugged and assaulted her in 1991, filming the incident without consent. Another woman, Liza Gardner, accused Combs of raping her and a friend when she was 16. These lawsuits were filed before the New York Adult Survivors Act expired, allowing claims despite statute limitations. Combs denied all accusations, calling them a "money grab."

December 2023 - Underage Sex Claim

In December, a woman, identified only as Jane Doe, filed a lawsuit accusing Sean "Diddy" Combs, former Bad Boy Records president Harve Pierre, and another man of "sex trafficking" and "gang rape" in 2003 when she was 17. She claimed that she was given excessive drugs and alcohol before the attack, leaving her in severe pain and with little memory of how she returned home. Combs denied the accusations, stating he did not commit the alleged acts, while Pierre called the claims "false" and motivated by financial gain.

December 2023 - Diddy's Denial

On December 6, Sean "Diddy" Combs broke his silence regarding the wave of lawsuits against him by posting a statement on Instagram. He declared, "ENOUGH IS ENOUGH," expressing frustration over what he described as attempts to damage his character, reputation, and legacy. He labeled the allegations as "sickening" and driven by financial motives, asserting his innocence and vowing to defend his name, family, and the truth. Combs emphasized his resolve to fight back against the claims being made against him.

February 2024 - Accusations of Grooming

In February 2024, music producer Rodney Jones Jr., who contributed to *The Love Album* in 2023, filed a lawsuit against Sean "Diddy" Combs. Jones accused Combs of making unwanted sexual advances and coercing him into hiring and engaging in sexual acts with prostitutes. He also alleged that Combs attempted to "groom" him into having sex with another man, claiming it was common in the music industry. In response, Combs' lawyer, Shawn Holley, dismissed the claims as lies and "pure fiction," citing proof that would discredit the allegations.

17 May 2024 - Cassie Assault Video Leaked

In 2016, CCTV footage surfaced showing Sean "Diddy" Combs physically assaulting Cassie Ventura in a Los Angeles hotel hallway. The video, aired by CNN, depicted Combs shoving Cassie to the ground, kicking her, and attempting to drag her by her shirt while throwing an object at her. Following the video's release, Combs issued an apology, stating, "I take full responsibility for my actions," expressing disgust at his behavior. Cassie later reflected on the lasting effects of domestic violence, saying the incident deeply affected her sense of self.

21 May 2024 - Former Model Sues

In 2003, model and actress Crystal McKinney accused Sean "Diddy" Combs of drugging her and coercing her into performing oral sex at a New York City recording studio. Shortly after, April Lampros filed a separate lawsuit, alleging four instances of sexual assault by Combs between 1995 and 2000. Lampros, who met Combs while studying at the Fashion Institute of Technology, claimed their romantic relationship quickly became abusive. She alleged that Combs once forced her to take ecstasy and engage in sexual activity with his then-girlfriend.

July 2024 - Combs Maintains Innocence Amid Eighth Lawsuit

In July, former adult film star Adria English filed a lawsuit accusing Sean "Diddy" Combs of grooming her for sex trafficking at parties between 2004 and 2009. Combs' attorney, Jonathan Davis, strongly denied the claims, insisting the allegations were unfounded and driven by financial motives.

September 10, 2024 - Court No-Show

Combs failed to appear at a virtual hearing for a lawsuit filed by Michigan inmate Derrick Lee Cardello-Smith, who accused him of drugging and assaulting him at a 1997 party in Detroit. As a result, a default judgment of $100 million was initially awarded to Cardello-Smith. However, the ruling was later overturned after Combs' legal team filed an appeal.

September 11, 2024 - Lawsuit by Girl Band Star

Dawn Richard, a former member of the girl group Danity Kane, also sued Combs, accusing him of repeated sexual assault and verbal abuse. She alleged that Combs had overworked and mistreated her while they were in the band Diddy Dirty Money.

September 16, 2024 - Combs' Arrest

Combs was taken into custody at a hotel in Manhattan after a grand jury issued an indictment against him. His legal team maintained that he had been cooperative with authorities and had voluntarily relocated to New York in preparation for the charges. His lawyer emphasized that these were the actions of an innocent man, looking forward to clearing his name in court.

September 17, 2024 - Charges and 'Freak Offs' Details Unveiled

Combs appeared in a New York court to face charges of sex trafficking, racketeering, and transporting individuals for prostitution. The unsealed indictment also included allegations of kidnapping, forced labor, and bribery. Prosecutors claimed that Combs led a criminal enterprise that abused women, coercing them into drug-fueled sexual orgies—referred to as "freak offs"—with male prostitutes. These events, described as "elaborate and organized," allegedly involved drugs such as cocaine, methamphetamine, and oxycodone, along with travel and recovery arrangements for victims, including intravenous fluids.

Prosecutors further alleged that Combs recorded these encounters and used the footage to intimidate and silence his victims. If convicted, Combs could face a sentence ranging from 15 years to life in prison. However, his attorney, Marc Agnifilo, contested the charges, asserting that the "freak offs" were consensual and that the allegations didn't meet the threshold for sex trafficking.

CHAPTER 7

Legacy and Impact After Her Passing

Remembering Kim's Influence

Kim Porter's passing in 2018 left a deep void in both the entertainment industry and the lives of those who knew her personally. A model, actress, mother, and philanthropist, Kim's legacy is defined by her grace, strength, and devotion to her family. Her influence extended far beyond her career; she was a beacon of love and support to her children and an inspiration to many within the industry. Kim cultivated an environment of nurturing and empowerment, especially for women in entertainment, exemplifying what it meant to persevere with humility despite the challenges that fame brought. Her generosity and warmth were hallmarks of her character, leaving a lasting impact on everyone fortunate enough to have been part of her world.

Kim's influence on those around her was especially profound in her role as a mother. She was the anchor for her children, instilling in them the values of love, compassion, and resilience. Her nurturing spirit and desire to protect her family were evident in the way she raised her four children, Quincy, Christian, and her twin daughters D'Lila and Jessie. Even after her passing, her presence continues to be felt in their lives, as her legacy lives on through them. Kim's strength as a mother, friend, and partner made her an unforgettable figure whose memory continues to inspire countless individuals.

Continuing Her Work

In the wake of her passing, Kim's legacy is not only remembered but also carried forward through the initiatives and projects she championed. During her life, Kim was committed to helping those around her, from supporting rising stars in the industry to being a foundational figure for her friends and family. The empowerment of women in entertainment was a central part of her work, and this continues to resonate today.

Kim's family and close friends have dedicated themselves to keeping her memory alive by continuing the charitable efforts she believed in. Whether through supporting causes that empower women, focusing on initiatives that uplift children, or advocating for mental health, Kim's passion for making a difference in the world lives on. In particular, her work with *Three Brown Girls*, which she co-founded, serves as a lasting tribute to her mission of fostering talent and supporting entrepreneurial endeavors.

Her children also carry on her legacy by embracing the values she instilled in them. Through their own personal and professional journeys, they honor her memory, ensuring that the lessons of love, strength, and perseverance she taught them continue to guide their paths.

Kim's life was one of purpose, and her impact continues to echo through the lives she touched. From the way she embraced her role as a mother to her commitment to lifting others up, Kim's legacy remains a shining example of how to live a life of love, compassion, and resilience. Her memory will continue to inspire generations, and her influence will forever be felt in the hearts of those who knew her and the causes she believed in.

CONCLUSION

Kim Porter's life was marked by resilience, love, and an unwavering commitment to her family and friends. Despite the challenges she faced, she remained a beacon of strength, inspiring those around her with her kindness, generosity, and spirit. Her legacy continues through her children, her philanthropic efforts, and the countless lives she touched. Though she is no longer with us, the lessons she left behind—of perseverance, love, and the importance of family—will continue to inspire future generations. Kim's story is one of enduring grace and impact, a testament to a life lived with purpose and heart. Her influence will never be forgotten, and her memory remains a guiding light for those who knew and loved her.

Made in the USA
Columbia, SC
25 September 2024

42891005R00026